BEST OF
JAPAN

Masaki Ko

southwater

Contents

Introduction

Although Japanese restaurants have become highly fashionable in the West, many people have been afraid to try this exotic cuisine at home. Now, however, with an increasing number of specialist shops stocking imported ingredients, there is no reason why you should not succeed.

None of these recipes is difficult, although some take time to prepare. Step-by-step instructions and illustrations demystify the key techniques, and superb photographs inspire a genuinely Japanese elegance and style.

Fish features extensively because Japan consists of a series of islands and because meat was banned for 250 years. Similarly, superb vegetable dishes, some featuring edible seaweeds, are characteristic and tofu (soya beancurd), introduced from China, quickly acquired a Japanese flavour. It is only since 1867 that the country's unique meat dishes have developed. Soups are clear broths, and noodles and rice are staples. However, perhaps the best example of Japan's unique cuisine is sushi, mouth-watering little packets of rice and fish, flavoured with vinegar.

For these wonderful dishes, all you need are sharp knives, a steady hand, patience and, maybe, a little practice.

Ingredients

Flavourings & Seasonings:
Shoyu, soy sauce, is the best-known seasoning ingredient. There are several different types: usukuchi is light in colour and saltier than tamari, dark soy sauce, which is used as a dip for sashimi (sliced raw fish) and other dishes. Do not use Chinese soy sauce, which is much stronger. Sushi vinegar is a seasoned and sweetened vinegar product. Rice vinegar is pale in colour and delicately flavoured. Sake, rice wine, is available in many qualities. It is not necessary to buy expensive sake for cooking. Mirin is a sweet wine used for cooking.

Miso is a fermented soya bean paste: white miso has a lighter flavour than red, and dark brown miso is strongly flavoured. Tonkatsu sauce has a fruity flavour and is served with deep-fried pork and croquettes. Seven spice flavour or pepper, shichimi, is a chilli-based spice containing hemp, poppy, rape and sesame seeds, anise pepper leaves and tangerine peel. It is a popular ingredient in Japanese cooking.

The strongly flavoured bonito, related to the tuna, is used dried in thin flakes, known as katsuo-bushi, to flavour stock and season dishes. Wasabi is an extremely hot green horseradish. It is available as a paste or powder to which water is added.

Gari are pale pink ginger pickles, served with sushi or sashimi to refresh the palate. Umeboshi are small, red pickled plums with a sharp and salty taste. They are used as filling for onigiri, rice triangles.

Above: A range of flavouring ingredients used in Japanese cooking.

Above: A selection of Japanese vegetables, tofu and seaweed.

Tofu: Also known as beancurd, this soya product is high in protein and, while it has little flavour of its own, readily absorbs that of other ingredients. It is available in various forms: soft, firm, silken, grilled (known as yaki-tofu), fried or dried.

Noodles & Grains: Various types of noodles are used. Somen are wheat noodles, while hiritaki noodles are made from the starch of the devil's tongue plant, which is a root vegetable. Canned or packed in water, they are good for sukiyaki. Katakuri-ko is potato starch or flour. Cornflour may be used instead.

Vegetables & Seaweed:
Gobo, edible burdock, is a long, thin root vegetable. It may be soaked to remove the bitterness. The blue-green stems of Japanese spring onions, negi, are long and thick. Mooli, or daikon, is a long white radish. Black or white konnyaku is a cake also made from flour produced from the devil's tongue plant. Tear it, rather than cut it, before cooking so that it absorbs more flavour.

Shiitake mushrooms have a good flavour, especially dried. Use the soaking water for stock. Enoki have long thin stems and tiny white caps. They are crisp with a delicate flavour and are eaten raw or cooked.

Several varieties of dried seaweed are used. These include kombu, kelp (used to flavour stock and served as a vegetable), and nori, dried and processed laver. This is sold in paper-thin sheets, which are toasted and used as a sushi wrapping. Ready-toasted and seasoned sheets, yaki-nori, are also available. Wakame is used for salads.

Basic Recipes

Boiled Rice

Washing rice is important, as it improves the flavour.

Serves 4–6

INGREDIENTS
480 g/1 lb 1 oz/2⅓ cups rice
600 ml/1 pint/2½ cups water

1 Place the rice in a bowl. Pour over plenty of water, then quickly drain. Stir the grains well, firmly pressing the rice by hand. Pour plenty of water over the rice and quickly drain it away. Repeat this three or four times.

2 Then add plenty of water and stir two or three times. Drain and repeat another two or three times, until the water runs clear.

3 Drain the rice well through a strainer and leave it to drain for 30–60 minutes.

4 Transfer the rice to a rice cooker, add the measured water and switch on. Alternatively, use a deep saucepan, cover and place over a moderate heat until steam emerges. Reduce the heat and simmer for 10 minutes. Finally, cook over a high heat for 5 seconds.

5 When the rice is cooked, leave it to stand for 15 minutes, then remove the lid and stir the cooked rice once with a wet spatula.

Kombu Seaweed & Bonito Flake Stock

This stock, known as *Ichiban-dashi*, is used for delicately flavoured dishes.

Makes about 800 ml/ 27 fl oz/3½ cups

INGREDIENTS
10 x 15 cm/4 x 6 in piece dried kombu seaweed (about 10 g/¼ oz)
10–15 g/¼–½ oz bonito flakes

1 Wipe the kombu with a damp cloth and cut two slits in it with scissors. Soak the kombu in 900 ml/ 1½ pints/3¾ cups cold water for at least 30 minutes.

2 Heat the kombu in its water over moderate heat. Just before the water boils, remove the seaweed. Add the bonito flakes. Bring to the boil over high heat, then remove from the heat.

3 Leave until all the bonito flakes have sunk to the pan base. Line a strainer with kitchen paper or muslin. Place over a bowl, then strain the stock.

Instant Stock (Dashi)

For speed or convenience when you need a small amount of stock, granules are very good. They are available from Japanese stores. Follow the packet instructions.

Cucumber & Carrot Garnishes

These attractive vegetable decorations are quickly and easily prepared.

INGREDIENTS
½ cucumber
1 large carrot

1 To make the cucumber garnish, cut
a 7.5 cm/3 in piece of cucumber,
2 cm/¾ in wide. Make four even cuts
along its length, 12 mm/½ in in from
one end. Repeat with the other pieces
of cucumber.

2 Curl the second and fourth strips
towards the base to form an open loop
shape. The fringed piece of cucumber
can also be spread out to form an
attractive fan shape.

3 To make the carrot garnish, peel
the carrot and cut into 5 mm/¼ in
slices. Trim the slices into rectangles,
2 x 7.5 cm/¾ x 3 in. Make a 5 mm/
¼ in cut along one edge of the carrot
so that the strip is still joined.

4 Make a second cut in the other
direction, again so that the strip is
joined. Bend the two ends together, to
cross over. You can also use this technique on cucumber or lemon peel.

Shaped Sushi

This sushi is packed full of a variety of flavours, but with a heavy emphasis on seafood that will appeal to the Western palate.

Serves 4

INGREDIENTS
480 g/1 lb 1 oz/2⅓ cups Japanese rice,
    washed and drained for 1 hour
600 ml/1 pint/2½ cups water
30 ml/2 tbsp sake or dry white wine
wasabi paste
salt
soy sauce and gari,
    to serve

FOR THE SUSHI VINEGAR
60 ml/4 tbsp rice vinegar
15 ml/1 tbsp sugar

FOR THE SEAFOOD GARNISH
1 squid body sac, skinned
    (about 200 g/7 oz total weight)
1 boiled octopus tentacle
200 g/7 oz block tuna for sashimi
200 g/7 oz block salmon
    for sashimi
4 large raw prawns,
    heads removed

FOR THE MARINADE
15 ml/1 tbsp rice vinegar
5 ml/1 tsp sugar

FOR THE ROLLED OMELETTE
3 eggs
15 ml/1 tbsp each of sake or dry
    white wine, sugar and water
1 cm/½ in strips yaki-nori seaweed

1 Cook the rice, replacing 30 ml/ 2 tbsp of the measured cooking water with the sake or wine. Meanwhile, heat the ingredients for the sushi vinegar, adding 5 ml/1 tsp salt, stir well and cool. Add this to the hot cooked rice, and stir well with a spatula, at the same time fanning the rice constantly. Cover with a damp cloth and leave to cool.

2 Cut the squid into strips 2–3 cm/ ¾–1¼ in by 5 cm/2 in. Slice the octopus into strips of the same size. Cut the tuna and salmon into similar size pieces, but about 3 mm/⅛ in thick.

3 Thread the prawns on to bamboo skewers from tail to head. Boil for 1 minute, then remove the skewers and shells, leaving the tails intact. Slit each prawn along the belly, taking care not to cut right through, and remove the dark vein, then open it up like a book. Mix the marinade ingredients in a dish, adding a pinch of salt, add the prawns and leave for 10 minutes.

4 Make a rolled omelette with the ingredients listed, following the technique in Rolled Omelette but adding 2 ml/⅓ tsp salt. Cool, then slice into 5 mm/¼ in thick pieces.

5 Wet your hands, then shape about 15–20 g/½–¾ oz rice into a rectangle measuring 1 cm/½ in thick, 2 cm/¾ in wide and 5 cm/2 in long.

6 Repeat with the remaining rice. Use your finger to spread a little wasabi on the middle of the rice oblongs and lay the seafood on top. Do not add wasabi for egg sushi but tie together with the seaweed. Serve with soy sauce, and gari to cleanse the palate after each mouthful.

Simple Rolled Sushi

To perfect the art of rolling sushi in seaweed takes practice and there is no better way than by starting with this simple form.

Makes 12 rolls or 72 slices

INGREDIENTS
6 sheets yaki-nori seaweed
200 g/7 oz block tuna for sashimi
200 g/7 oz block salmon
    for sashimi
400 g/14 oz/2 cups Japanese rice, cooked
    as for Shaped Sushi, using Mixed
    Vinegar (see below)
wasabi paste
½ cucumber, quartered lengthways
    and seeds removed
gari, to garnish
soy sauce, to serve

FOR THE MIXED VINEGAR
45 ml/3 tbsp rice vinegar
15 ml/1 tbsp sugar
3 ml/⅔ tsp salt

1 Cut the nori sheets in half. Cut the tuna and salmon into four 1 cm/½ in square, long sticks. The sticks should be the same length as the long side of the nori. Use two sticks per nori if necessary.

2 Place a sheet of nori, shiny side downwards, on a bamboo mat on a chopping board.

3 Divide the rice in half, then mark each half into six, making 12 portions in all. Spread one portion of the rice over the nori with your fingers, leaving a 1 cm/½ in space uncovered at the top and bottom.

4 Spread a little wasabi in a horizontal line along the middle of the rice and lay a stick of tuna on this.

5 Holding the mat and the edge of the nori nearest to you, roll up the nori and rice into a tube. Use the mat as a guide – do not roll it into the food. Roll the rice tightly so that it sticks together and encloses the filling.

6 Carefully roll the sushi off the mat. Make 11 other rolls in the same way, four for each filling ingredient. Do not use wasabi with the cucumber. Use a wet knife to cut each roll into six slices and stand them on a platter. Wipe and re-rinse the knife occasionally between cuts. Garnish with gari and serve soy sauce with the sushi.

COOK'S TIP: Each individual sushi should be as neat and attractive as possible. They should be arranged in an orderly pattern as best suited to the serving plate or dish.

Tofu-wrapped Sushi

This is a popular picnic dish, particularly with children, who like its slightly sweet flavour. The tofu should be prepared while the rice filling is still being cooked.

Makes 12

INGREDIENTS
6 sheets fried tofu
200 ml/7 fl oz/scant 1 cup
    Kombu Seaweed & Bonito Flake Stock
    or instant dashi
45 ml/3 tbsp sugar
35 ml/7 tsp soy sauce
30 ml/2 tbsp sake or dry
    white wine
30 ml/2 tbsp mirin
dash of rice vinegar
gari, to garnish

FOR THE RICE
240 g/8½ oz/1⅛ cups Japanese rice
300 ml/½ pint/1¼ cups water
15 ml/1 tbsp sake

FOR THE SUSHI VINEGAR
30 ml/2 tbsp rice vinegar
15 ml/1 tbsp sugar
2.5 ml/½ tsp salt

1 Lay the tofu on a board. Using a chopstick as a rolling pin, roll each sheet to ensure that they open easily when boiled. Bring a large saucepan of water to the boil and blanch the tofu, then drain and squeeze. Cut the sheets of tofu in half widthways, then carefully open out with a knife to make 12 small sacks or pockets.

2 Bring the stock or instant dashi, sugar, soy sauce, sake or dry white wine, mirin and rice vinegar to the boil. Add the tofu, cover with folded foil and simmer until the liquid has virtually evaporated, pressing the foil down occasionally to squeeze the soup from the tofu and prevent the pockets from filling. Drain and cool.

3 Heat the rice vinegar, sugar and salt for the sushi vinegar together in a small saucepan. When the sugar and salt have dissolved, remove the pan from the heat and set aside to cool.

COOK'S TIP: You can buy sheets of fried tofu in Japanese grocers. They can be kept for a short while in the freezer, but do not keep for very long in the fridge.

4 Cook the rice, replacing 15 ml/
1 tbsp of the measured cooking water
with the sake. Add the sushi vinegar to
the rice and stir well with a spatula.
Divide the warm rice between the
tofu and fold the tofu to enclose the
rice in neat parcels. Arrange on plates
with the folded sides underneath and
serve garnished with gari.

Rolled Sushi with Mixed Filling

This wonderful mix of seafood, shiitake mushrooms and vegetables typifies the sophisticated balance of flavours in traditional sushi recipes.

Makes 32 pieces

INGREDIENTS
4 large dried shiitake mushrooms
1 small carrot, quartered lengthways
1 chikuwa fish cake or 4 crab sticks, cut into strips as for the carrot
4 sheets yaki-nori seaweed
320 g/11½ oz/1½ cups Japanese rice, cooked as for Shaped Sushi, using Mixed Vinegar (see below)
½ cucumber, quartered lengthways, seeds removed
soy sauce and gari, to serve

FOR THE SEASONING
35 ml/7 tsp soy sauce
15 ml/1 tbsp each of sake or dry white wine, mirin and sugar

FOR THE ROLLED OMELETTE
2 eggs
10 ml/2 tsp sugar
pinch of salt

FOR THE MIXED VINEGAR
40 ml/8 tsp rice vinegar
22.5 ml/4½ tsp sugar
3 ml/⅗ tsp salt

1 Soak the shiitake in 200 ml/7 fl oz/ scant 1 cup water for 30 minutes. Drain, reserving the stock, and remove their stems. Pour the stock into a saucepan, add the seasonings and simmer the carrot, mushrooms and crab sticks for 4–5 minutes.

2 Remove the carrot and chikuwa or crab sticks. Cook the shiitake until the liquid has evaporated, then slice them. Make the rolled omelette following the technique for Rolled Omelette.

3 Place a bamboo mat on a chopping board. Lay a sheet of nori, shiny side down, on the mat.

4 Spread a quarter of the prepared dressed rice over the nori using your fingers, leaving a 1 cm/½ in space at the top and bottom. Place a quarter of each of the filling ingredients across the middle of the rice.

5 Carefully hold the nearest edge of the nori and the mat, then roll up the nori using the mat as a guide to make a neat tube of rice with the filling ingredients in the middle. Roll the rice tightly to ensure that the grains stick together and to keep the filling in place. Roll the sushi off the mat and make three more rolls in the same way.

6 Using a wet knife, cut each roll into eight pieces and stand them upright on a platter. Serve soy sauce and gari with the sushi.

COOK'S TIP: Chikuwa fish cakes are available ready-cooked fresh or frozen from Japanese supermarkets.

Serve-yourself Sushi

Diners select their favourite fillings in this fun dish, *Temaki-zushi*.

Serves 4

INGREDIENTS
480 g/1 lb 1 oz/2⅓ cups Japanese rice,
    cooked as for Shaped Sushi, using Mixed
    Vinegar (see below)
10 sheets yaki-nori seaweed, quartered
wasabi
mayonnaise
soy sauce, to serve

FOR THE MIXED VINEGAR
60 ml/4 tbsp rice vinegar
30 ml/2 tbsp sugar
5 ml/1 tsp salt

FOR THE ROLLED OMELETTE
2 large eggs
10 ml/2 tsp sugar
pinch of salt

FOR THE FILLINGS
115 g/4 oz block tuna for sashimi
115 g/4 oz block salmon for sashimi
4–8 crab sticks
1 squid body sac, skinned (about 200 g/7 oz
    total weight)
½ cucumber, seeds removed
1 avocado, halved, stoned and peeled
juice of ½ lemon
4–8 raw tiger prawns, prepared as for
    Shaped Sushi
60 ml/4 tbsp salmon roe
½ round lettuce, separated into leaves
punnet of cress, trimmed

1 Make one rolled omelette, using the ingredients listed, following the technique for Rolled Omelette.

2 Use a sharp knife to slice the tuna, salmon, crab sticks and squid into 1 cm/½ in wide long strips.

3 Cut the cucumber, avocado and omelette into similar-size strips. Sprinkle lemon juice on the avocado to stop it from turning brown.

4 Place all the filling ingredients on serving platters, the cooked rice in a bowl, the quartered yaki-nori seaweed on a separate plate, and the wasabi, mayonnaise and soy sauce in dishes.

5 Each guest takes a piece of seaweed and lays it flat with the shiny side facing downwards. About 15 ml/1 tbsp rice is placed on it and spread evenly with the fingers. Filling ingredients to taste are placed neatly on the middle of the rice in strips, wasabi or mayonnaise added to taste and the nori rolled up into small tubes. The impromptu sushi are then dipped in soy sauce.

Sliced Raw Salmon

Sashimi

Salmon is a good choice for those who have not tried sashimi before as most people are familiar with smoked salmon, which is uncooked.

Serves 4

INGREDIENTS
2 fresh salmon fillets, skinned and
   any bones removed
   (about 400 g/14 oz total weight)
soy sauce,
   to serve

FOR THE GARNISH
50 g/2 oz/¼ cup mooli
wasabi paste
shiso leaf or fresh basil

2 Finely shred the mooli, place in a bowl of cold water and leave for 5 minutes, then drain well.

1 Put the salmon fillets in a freezer for 10 minutes to make them easier to cut, then lay them skinned side up with the thick end to your right and away from you. Use a long sharp knife and tilt it to the left. Slice carefully towards you, starting the cut from the point of the knife, then slide the slice away from the fillet, to the right. Always slice from the far side towards you.

3 Place three slices of salmon on a plate, then overlap another two slices on them diagonally. You can arrange fewer or more slices per portion, but an odd number looks better.

VARIATIONS: All kinds of fresh fish can be used for sashimi: monkfish, tuna and cod are all excellent choices.

4 Garnish with the mooli, wasabi and shiso leaf, then serve immediately with a small bowl of soy sauce.

COOK'S TIP: This technique for slicing raw fish is known as *hira zukuri* and works well with most firm-fleshed fish. However, it is essential to use a razor-sharp knife with a long blade.

Teriyaki Trout

Teriyaki sauce is very useful, not only for fish, as here, but also for meat, such as steak or chicken.

Serves 4

INGREDIENTS
4 trout fillets

FOR THE MARINADE
75 ml/5 tbsp soy sauce
75 ml/5 tbsp sake or dry white wine
75 ml/5 tbsp mirin

1 Lay the trout fillets in a shallow dish in a single layer. Mix the ingredients for the marinade and pour the marinade over the fish. Cover and marinate in the fridge for 5–6 hours, turning occasionally.

> COOK'S TIP: To make a teriyaki barbecue sauce, heat the marinade until boiling, then reduce it until it thickens. When you grill the fish or meat, brush it with the sauce several times as it cooks.

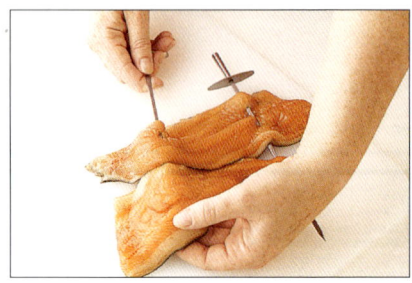

2 Thread two trout fillets neatly together on two metal skewers. Repeat with the remaining two fillets. You could cut the fillets in half if they are too big.

3 Grill the trout on both sides on a barbecue, over a high heat. Keep the skewered fish about 10 cm/4 in away from the flame and brush it with the marinade several times. Grill until both sides are shiny and the trout is cooked through, about 12 minutes.

4 Slide the trout off the skewers while it is hot. Serve hot or cold with any remaining marinade.

VARIATION: If you prefer, the trout may be cooked under a conventional grill instead of on a barbecue.

Assorted Tempura

This is a wonderfully delicate dish of savoury fritters in light batter. The secret of success is to use really cold water.

Serves 4–6

INGREDIENTS
115 g/4 oz finely grated mooli (optional)
8 raw tiger prawns, peeled,
    heads removed, but with
    tails intact
flour, for coating
½ squid body sac, cut into 3 cm/1¼ in
    thick strips
115 g/4 oz sweet potato, unpeeled,
    sliced and soaked in cold water for
    5 minutes
75 g/3 oz carrot, cut
    into matchsticks
4 shiitake mushrooms,
    stems removed
50 g/2 oz/¾ cup French
    beans, trimmed
1 red pepper, seeded and sliced into
    2 cm/¾ in strips
oil, for deep frying

FOR THE TEMPURA DIP
200 ml/7 fl oz/scant 1 cup water
45 ml/3 tbsp mirin
6 g/¼ oz bonito flakes
45 ml/3 tbsp soy sauce

FOR THE TEMPURA BATTER
½ egg (see method)
90 ml/6 tbsp iced water
75 g/3 oz/⅔ cup plain flour
2.5 ml/½ tsp baking powder
2 ice cubes

1 Make the dip. Put the ingredients in a pan and bring to the boil. Remove from the heat, cool and then strain. Divide among four small bowls. Place the grated mooli, if using, in a sieve to drain.

2 Cut a diagonal slit through each prawn tail. Press out excess water. Make a shallow cut down the back of each prawn and remove the black vein. Lay a prawn on its back. Make three or four diagonal slits into the flesh, about two-thirds of the way in towards the back, leaving the pieces attached. Repeat with the others and flatten them with your fingers.

3 Start heating the oil to 185°C/365°F. Meanwhile, make the batter. Stir, but do not beat the egg in a bowl and set half aside for another use. Add the water, flour and baking powder. Stir two or three times only, leaving some free flour unblended and ignoring any lumps. Add the ice cubes.

4 Dust the prawns lightly with flour. Holding them by the tail, quickly dip them into the batter, a few at a time, then slowly lower them into the oil. Fry all the prawns and the squid in this way until crisp but not golden. Drain well and lower the temperature of the oil to 170°C/340°F.

5 Dip the vegetables straight into the batter and cook in the same way. Dip the carrot sticks and beans in small bunches. Dip only the undersides of the mushrooms. Drain well. If the batter begins to thin, sprinkle 15 ml/ 1 tbsp flour over it without mixing. Place the tempura on a plate and serve immediately with the dip.

Fried Swordfish

This is a light and tasty cold dish that is suitable for serving on a hot summer's day.

Serves 4

INGREDIENTS
4 swordfish steaks, boned, skin left on
    (about 600 g/1 lb 5 oz total weight)
15 ml/1 tbsp soy sauce
7.5 ml/1½ tsp rice vinegar
bunch of spring onions
4 asparagus spears, trimmed
30 ml/2 tbsp vegetable oil

FOR THE MARINADE
45 ml/3 tbsp soy sauce
45 ml/3 tbsp rice vinegar
30 ml/2 tbsp sake or dry
    white wine
15 ml/1 tbsp sugar
15 ml/1 tbsp instant dashi
    or water
7.5 ml/1½ tsp sesame oil

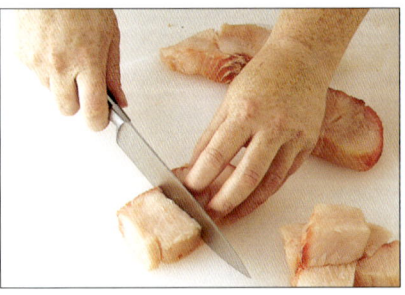

1 Cut the swordfish steaks into 4 cm/ 1½ in chunks and place in a dish. Pour the soy sauce and 7.5 ml/1½ tsp rice vinegar over the fish, then set aside for 5 minutes.

2 Meanwhile, cut the spring onions into 3 cm/1¼ in lengths and the asparagus into 4 cm/1½ in lengths.

3 Mix the ingredients for the marinade in a dish. Heat three-quarters of the vegetable oil in a frying pan. Wipe the swordfish with kitchen paper and fry over a moderate heat for about 1–2 minutes on each side, or until cooked. Remove the fish from the frying pan and place it in the prepared marinade.

4 Clean the frying pan and heat the remaining oil in it. Fry the spring onions over a moderate heat until browned, then add them to the fish.

5 Fry the asparagus in the oil remaining in the pan over a low heat for 3–4 minutes, then add to the fish.

COOK'S TIPS: It is important to wipe the marinated swordfish pieces with kitchen paper before placing them in the hot oil. Wet fish causes steam which impedes the searing process. You might also find it better to cook the fish in batches, as overcrowding also prevents successful searing.

6 Leave the fish and vegetables to marinate for 10–20 minutes, turning the pieces occasionally. Serve the cold fish and vegetables with the marinade on a large, deep plate.

VARIATION: This dish is equally successful made with other types of firm white fish. Shark steaks, for example, make a good alternative.

Yakitori Chicken

Yakitori are Japanese-style chicken kebabs. They are easy to eat and ideal for barbecues or parties.

Serves 4

INGREDIENTS
bunch of spring onions
6 boneless chicken thighs
   (with skin)
seven flavour spice,
   to serve

FOR THE YAKITORI SAUCE
150 ml/¼ pint/⅔ cup
   soy sauce
90 g/3½ oz/½ cup sugar
25 ml/5 tsp sake or dry
   white wine
15 ml/1 tbsp plain flour

1 To make the sauce, stir the soy sauce, sugar and sake or wine into the flour in a small saucepan and bring to the boil, stirring. Reduce the heat and simmer for 10 minutes, until the sauce is reduced by one-third. Then set aside.

2 Cut the spring onions into 3 cm/1¼ in long pieces. Cut each chicken thigh into six chunks.

3 Thread the chicken and spring onions alternately on to 12 bamboo skewers. Grill under a medium heat or on the barbecue for 5–10 minutes, brushing generously several times with the sauce, until the chicken is cooked but still moist.

VARIATION: If you prefer, you can substitute boneless chicken breasts for the thighs used here.

4 Serve with a little extra yakitori sauce, offering seven flavour spice with the kebabs.

COOK'S TIP: Seven flavour spice, a variety of a spicy condiment called *togarashi*, is a most interesting accompaniment for this dish.

Chicken & Egg with Rice

Oyako-don, the Japanese name, means parent (*oya*), child (*ko*) and bowl (*don*) because it uses both chicken meat and egg.

Serves 4

INGREDIENTS
300 g/11 oz boneless chicken thighs
1 large mild onion,
    thinly sliced
200 ml/7 fl oz/scant 1 cup
    Kombu Seaweed & Bonito Flake Stock
    or instant dashi
20 ml/4 tsp sugar
60 ml/4 tbsp soy sauce
30 ml/2 tbsp mirin
4–6 large eggs, beaten
60 ml/4 tbsp frozen
    peas, thawed
1 kg/2¼ lb/7 cups freshly
    boiled rice (450g/1 lb/3½ cups raw)
½ sheet yaki-nori seaweed, shredded,
    to garnish

1 With a sharp knife, slice the chicken diagonally into strips about 1½ cm/½ in thick, then cut it into 3 cm/1¼ in lengths.

2 Place the onion, stock, sugar, soy sauce and mirin in a saucepan and bring to the boil. Add the chicken and cook over a moderate heat for about 5 minutes, or until the chicken is cooked. Skim any scum off the surface.

3 Ladle a quarter of the mixture into a frying pan and bring to the boil.

4 Pour a quarter of the egg over the mixture in the frying pan and add a quarter of the peas. Cover and cook over a moderate heat until the egg is set as preferred.

5 Spoon a quarter of the rice into an individual bowl and slide the egg mixture on top. Prepare the remaining portions in the same way. Serve hot, sprinkled with the yaki-nori seaweed.

VARIATION: You could substitute other green vegetables for the peas, such as small florets of lightly steamed broccoli.

Deep Fried Pork Strips with Shredded Cabbage

Deep fried pork is very tasty when served with light green cabbage and a fruity sauce, known as *tonkatsu*. This dish is enjoyed throughout Japan.

Serves 4

INGREDIENTS
4 boneless pork loin steaks (115 g/4 oz each)
7.5 ml/1½ tsp salt
plain flour, for coating
2 eggs, very lightly beaten
50 g/2 oz/1 cup fresh white breadcrumbs
½ light green cabbage, finely shredded
oil, for deep frying
freshly ground black pepper

FOR THE SAUCE
100 ml/3½ fl oz/generous ⅓ cup fruity
   brown sauce
45 ml/3 tbsp tomato ketchup
15 ml/1 tbsp sugar

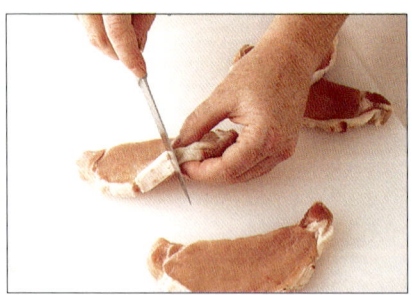

1 Cut through any fat on the pork steaks to ensure they remain flat when frying. Beat the pork with a meat mallet or rolling pin to tenderize it. Season with the salt and pepper to taste, and dust lightly with flour.

2 Dip the pork steaks into the lightly beaten egg first and then coat with the breadcrumbs. Press the breadcrumbs on to the steaks with your fingers to ensure they stick well. Chill for about 10 minutes.

3 Meanwhile, soak the shredded cabbage in cold water for about 5 minutes. Drain well and chill until you are ready to serve. Mix the ingredients for the sauce, stirring until the sugar has dissolved.

4 Heat the oil to 165–170°C/ 330–340°F. Deep-fry two steaks at a time for about 6 minutes, turning them until they are crisp and golden. Skim any floating breadcrumbs from the oil occasionally to prevent them from burning. Drain the steaks well and keep hot.

COOK'S TIP: Commercial Japanese *tonkatsu* sauce is available ready prepared from Oriental supermarkets and it may be substituted for the ingredients listed here, if preferred.

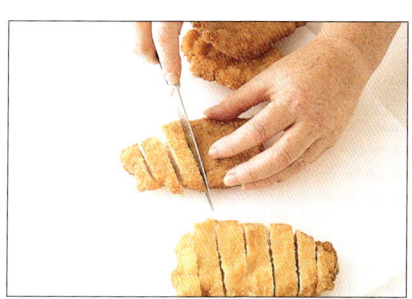

5 Cut the pork steaks into 2 cm/
¾ in strips and place on a plate.
Arrange the cabbage beside the pork
and pour the sauce over the pork.
Serve immediately.

Vegetable-stuffed Beef Rolls

Thinly sliced meats are used very widely in Japanese cooking, so there are countless recipes for them. These stuffed beef rolls are very popular for picnic meals.

Serves 4

INGREDIENTS
50 g/2 oz carrot
50 g/2 oz green pepper, seeded
bunch of spring onions
400 g/14 oz beef topside,
   thinly sliced
plain flour, for dusting
15 ml/1 tbsp oil
parsley sprigs, to garnish

FOR THE SAUCE
30 ml/2 tbsp sugar
45 ml/3 tbsp soy sauce
45 ml/3 tbsp mirin

2 The beef slices should be no more than 2 mm/¹⁄₁₂ in thick and about 15 cm/6 in x 7.5 cm/3 in oblongs. Lay a slice of beef on a board and top with carrot, green pepper and spring onion strips. Roll up quite tightly and dust lightly with flour. Repeat with the remaining beef and vegetables.

1 Shred the carrot and green pepper into 4–5 cm/1½–2 in lengths. Halve the spring onions lengthways, then shred the halves diagonally into 4–5 cm/1½–2 in lengths.

3 Heat the oil in a frying pan. Add the beef rolls, placing the joins underneath to prevent them from unrolling. Fry over a moderate heat until browned and cooked, turning occasionally.

4 Add the sugar, soy sauce and mirin for the sauce and increase the heat. Roll the beef slices quickly to glaze the rolls.

5 Remove the rolls from the pan and halve them, cutting at a slant. Stand the rolls on a plate, with the sloping cut end facing upwards. Dress with the sauce and garnish with parsley. Serve hot or cold.

Sukiyaki

You will need a chafing dish and burner or portable gas or electric cooker for this dish as it is cooked at the table.

Serves 4

INGREDIENTS
1 kg/2¼ lb beef topside, very thinly sliced
25 g/1 oz lard, for cooking
4 leeks or Japanese spring onions,
    sliced diagonally into pieces
    1 cm/½ in thick
bunch of shungiku or spinach leaves, stems
    removed and coarsely chopped (optional)
bunch of enoki mushrooms, brown roots
    cut off (optional)
8 shiitake mushrooms, stems removed
300 g/11 oz shirataki noodles, boiled for
    2 minutes, drained and halved
2 blocks yaki-tofu,
    cut into 3 cm/1¼ in cubes
4–8 eggs, to serve

FOR THE SUKIYAKI STOCK
100 ml/3½ fl oz/generous ⅓ cup mirin
45 ml/3 tbsp sugar
100 ml/3½ fl oz/generous ⅓ cup
    soy sauce

FOR THE SEASONING
200 ml/7 fl oz/scant 1 cup Kombu Seaweed
    & Bonito Flake Stock or instant dashi
100 ml/3½ fl oz/generous ⅓ cup sake
15 ml/1 tbsp soy sauce

1 To make the stock, bring the mirin to the boil. Add the sugar and soy sauce and bring to the boil again, then remove from the heat and set aside.

2 To make the seasoning, bring the stock, sake and soy sauce to the boil, then remove from the heat. Set aside.

3 Arrange the separated beef slices on a large serving plate with the lard. Place all the remaining ingredients on large plates. Beat the eggs and divide among four small bowls.

4 Stand the portable cooker on a heavy mat. Melt the lard, add three or four slices of beef and some leeks or spring onions, and then pour in the sukiyaki stock. Gradually add all the remaining ingredients, except the eggs, to the cooker.

5 Place a bowl of egg in front of each person. When the beef and vegetables are cooked, diners help themselves to the ingredients and dip them in the raw egg.

6 Gradually add the seasoning when the sukiyaki stock has thickened and carry on cooking until the ingredients have all been used. If required, add additional sugar and soy sauce to taste for extra flavour.

Mooli with Sesame Miso Sauce

The simple elegance of this vegetable dish makes it a good choice of starter to serve at a dinner party.

Serves 4

INGREDIENTS
1 medium mooli, about 800 g/1¾ lb
15 ml/1 tbsp rice, washed
1 sheet kombu seaweed
   (20 x 10 cm/8 x 4 in)
salt
punnet of cress, to garnish

FOR THE SESAME MISO SAUCE
75 g/3 oz/generous ⅓ cup
   red miso
75 g/3 oz/generous ⅓ cup
   white miso
60 ml/4 tbsp mirin
30 ml/2 tbsp sugar
20 ml/4 tsp ground white
   sesame seeds

1 Slice the mooli into 2 cm/¾ in thick slices, then peel off the skin. Wrap the rice in a piece of muslin or cheesecloth and tie it with string, allowing room for expansion.

2 Place the mooli in a saucepan and fill with water. Add the rice bag and a little salt, bring to the boil, then simmer for 15 minutes. Gently drain the mooli and discard the rice.

3 Place the seaweed in a large shallow pan, lay the mooli on top and fill with water. Bring to the boil, then simmer for 20 minutes.

4 Meanwhile, make the sauce. Mix the red and white miso pastes well in a saucepan. Add the mirin and sugar, then simmer for 5–6 minutes, stirring continuously. Remove from the heat and add the sesame seeds.

5 Arrange the mooli and seaweed in a large dish with their cooking stock. Sprinkle cress over the top. Serve the mooli on small plates with the sesame miso sauce poured over and garnished with some of the cress. The seaweed is used only to flavour the mooli, it is not eaten.

COOK'S TIP: The small bag of uncooked rice is added to the cooking water to keep the mooli white during cooking and remove any bitterness from the vegetable.

Spinach with Bonito Flakes

This is a cold side dish. A vegetarian version can be prepared by omitting the bonito flakes and marinating the spinach in the Kombu Seaweed Stock and soy sauce.

Serves 4

INGREDIENTS
300 g/11 oz whole spinach,
    roots trimmed
60 ml/4 tbsp fine bonito flakes

FOR THE MARINADE
60 ml/4 tbsp Kombu Seaweed & Bonito
    Flake Stock or instant dashi
20 ml/4 tsp usukuchi soy sauce

1 Wash the spinach thoroughly. Keep the stems together, then hold the leaves of the spinach and lower the stems into boiling water for 10 seconds before lowering the leaves into the water and boiling for 1–2 minutes. Do not overcook the spinach.

2 Meanwhile, prepare a large bowl of cold water. Drain the spinach and soak it in the cold water for 1 minute to preserve its green colour and remove any bitterness.

3 Drain the spinach and squeeze it well, holding the stems upwards and squeezing firmly down the length of the leaves.

4 Mix the stock and soy sauce in a dish and marinate the spinach in this mixture for 10–15 minutes, turning it over once.

COOK'S TIP: Japanese spinach beet has red stalks, and is similar to the *pallack* spinach sold in West Indian markets. Ordinary fresh spinach works just as well, however.

5 Squeeze the spinach lightly and cut it into 3–4 cm/1¼–1½ in long pieces, reserving the marinade. Divide the spinach among four small bowls, arranging the pieces so that the cut edges face upwards. Sprinkle 15 ml/ 1 tbsp bonito flakes and a little of the marinade over each portion, then serve the dish immediately.

Rolled Omelette

This is a firmly set, rolled omelette, which is cut into neat pieces and is delicious either on its own or with rice.

Serves 4

INGREDIENTS
8 eggs
60 ml/4 tbsp sugar
20 ml/4 tsp soy sauce, plus extra
    to serve
90 ml/6 tbsp sake or dry white wine
vegetable oil, for frying

FOR THE GARNISH
8 cm/3¼ in length of mooli,
    finely grated
shiso leaves
gari

1 Break the eggs into a large bowl. Mix them together by stirring using a pair of chopsticks with a cutting, figure-of-eight action.

2 Mix the sugar with the soy sauce and sake or dry white wine. Lightly stir this mixture into the eggs. Pour half the mixture into another bowl for cooking in two equal batches.

3 Heat a little oil in a frying pan and wipe off the excess. Pour a quarter of the mixture from one bowl into the pan, tilting the pan to coat it. When the edge has set, but the middle is moist, roll up the egg towards you.

4 Moisten kitchen paper with oil and grease the empty side of the pan. Pour a third of the remaining egg from the first bowl into the pan. Lift the rolled egg with your chopsticks and let the raw egg run underneath it. When the edge has set, roll up the omelette in the opposite direction.

5 Slide the roll towards you again, grease the pan and pour half of the remaining mixture on to it, allowing the egg to run under the roll as before. Repeat step 4 with the remaining egg mixture. Cook for 10 seconds.

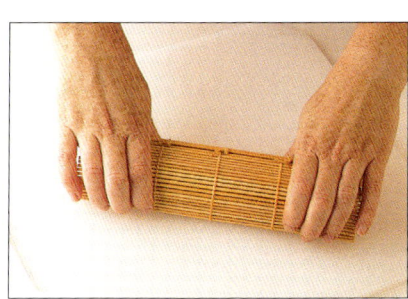

6 Slide the omelette out on to a bamboo mat and roll the mat tightly to retain the omelette's shape, then press neatly into a rectangle. Leave to cool. Cook the second batch of egg mixture in the same way. Slice the cold omelettes into 2.5 cm/1 in thick pieces and garnish with mooli, shiso and gari. Serve with soy sauce.

Deep Fried Tofu & Asparagus in Stock

Agedashi is the name for dishes of deep fried (*age*) ingredients served in a stock (*dashi*) or thin sauce.

Serves 4

INGREDIENTS
about ½ packet fresh Japanese tofu
 (10 x 5 x 3 cm/4 x 2 x 1¼ in),
 200 g/7 oz weighed without water
4 asparagus spears, trimmed of tough
 stalk ends
1 beefsteak tomato, skinned
oil, for deep frying
cornflour, for coating

FOR THE SAUCE
200 ml/7 fl oz/scant 1 cup instant dashi
50 ml/2 fl oz/¼ cup mirin
50 ml/2 fl oz/¼ cup soy sauce

1 Wrap the tofu in a clean dish towel and press it between two plates for 30 minutes to remove excess moisture. Alternatively, wrap the tofu in kitchen paper on a plate and cook in the microwave for 1 minute (600W) to remove excess water.

2 Cut the tofu into eight cubes (about 2.5 cm/1 in each). Cut the asparagus into 3–4 cm/1¼–1½ in lengths. Halve and seed the tomato, then cut it into 5 mm/¼ in cubes.

3 Heat the oil for deep frying to 170°C/340°F. Coat the tofu cubes with cornflour.

4 Deep-fry the pieces in two batches over a medium heat for 7–10 minutes, until cooked through and golden. Drain well.

5 Meanwhile, place the ingredients for the sauce in a pan and bring to the boil, then simmer for 3 minutes. Deep fry the asparagus for 2 minutes and drain well.

6 Place the tofu on a large plate and arrange the asparagus on top. Pour on the hot sauce and sprinkle the tomato on top. Serve immediately.

Winter Tofu & Vegetables

This dish is brought bubbling hot to the table with a bowl of dip to accompany the freshly cooked tofu and vegetables.

Serves 4

INGREDIENTS
1 sheet kombu seaweed
   (20 x 10 cm/8 x 4 in)
2 packets Japanese silken tofu
   (each 10 x 8 x 3 cm/4 x 3¼ x 1¼ in),
   about 600 g/1 lb 5 oz
2 leeks
4 shiitake mushrooms, stems removed
   and cross cut in top
spring onions, chopped, to garnish

FOR THE DIP
200 ml/7 fl oz/scant 1 cup soy sauce
generous 15 ml/1 tbsp mirin
100 ml/3½ fl oz/generous ⅓ cup
   bonito flakes

1 Half fill a large flameproof casserole or saucepan with cold water and soak the sheet of kombu seaweed in it for 30 minutes.

2 Cut the tofu into 4 cm/1½ in cubes. Slice the leeks diagonally into 2 cm/¾ in thick slices.

3 To make the dip, bring the soy sauce and mirin to the boil, then add the bonito flakes. Remove from the heat and leave until all the flakes have sunk to the bottom of the pan, then strain the sauce and pour it into a small heatproof basin.

4 Stand the basin in the middle of the saucepan containing the kombu stock, placing it on an upturned saucer, if necessary, so that it is well above the level of the stock. This keeps the dip hot. Bring the stock to the boil. Add the mushrooms and leeks, and cook over a moderate heat for about 5 minutes, until softened.

6 Take the pan to the table, spoon the dip into four small bowls and sprinkle the spring onions into the dip. Diners help themselves to tofu and vegetables from the pan and eat them with the dip. The kombu seaweed is used only to flavour the dish and is not eaten.

5 Then gently add the pieces of tofu. When the tofu starts floating, it is ready to eat.

Prawn & Egg-knot Soup

This delicately flavoured and elegant soup would be perfect served on any special occasion in the summer.

Serves 4

INGREDIENTS
800 ml/27 fl oz/3½ cups Kombu Seaweed &
   Bonito Flake Stock or instant dashi
dash of usukuchi soy sauce
2.5 ml/½ tsp sake or dry white wine
salt
1 spring onion, thinly sliced,
   to garnish

FOR THE PRAWN SHINJO BALLS
200 g/7 oz large raw prawns, peeled and
   deveined, thawed if frozen
65 g/2½ oz cod fillet, skinned
5 ml/1 tsp egg white
5 ml/1 tsp sake or dry white wine
20 ml/4 tsp cornflour or
   katakuri-ko
2.5 ml/½ tsp soy sauce

FOR THE OMELETTE
1 egg, beaten
dash of mirin
oil, for frying

1 Process the prawns, cod, egg white, 5 ml/1 tsp sake or wine, cornflour or katakuri-ko, soy sauce and a pinch of salt in a food processor or blender to make a sticky paste. Alternatively, finely chop the prawns and cod, crush them with the knife's blade and then pound them well in a mortar with a pestle, adding the remaining ingredients.

2 Shape the mixture into four balls and steam them for 10 minutes over a high heat. Soak the spring onion in cold water for 5 minutes, then drain.

3 Mix the egg with a pinch of salt and the mirin. Heat a little oil in a medium frying pan and pour in the beaten egg, tilting the pan to coat it evenly. When the egg has set, turn the omelette over and cook for 30 seconds. Leave to cool.

COOK'S TIP: The omelette can be made in advance and stored in the fridge until required.

4 Cut the omelette into long strips, 2 cm/¾ in wide. Knot each strip once, place in a strainer and rinse with hot water to remove excess oil. Bring the stock to the boil and add the usukuchi soy sauce, a pinch of salt and a dash of sake or wine. Divide the prawn balls and the egg knots among four bowls. Pour in the soup, sprinkle with the spring onion and serve.

Miso & Tofu Soup

In Japan, this is usually served with every meal that includes rice.

Serves 4

INGREDIENTS
½ packet silken tofu
   (10 x 5 x 3 cm/4 x 2 x 1¼ in), about
   150 g/5 oz weighed without water
800 ml/27 fl oz/3½ cups Kombu Seaweed &
   Bonito Flake Stock or instant dashi
6 g/¼ oz dried wakame seaweed
60 ml/4 tbsp white or red miso
2 spring onions, chopped,
   to garnish

1 Cut the tofu into 1 cm/½ in cubes. Bring the stock to the boil and reduce the heat.

2 Add the wakame and simmer for 1–2 minutes. Pour some soup into a bowl and add the miso, stirring so that it dissolves. Pour the mixture back into the pan.

3 Add the tofu and heat through for 1 minute, then serve immediately. Garnish with chopped spring onions.

COOK'S TIP: Reduce the heat when the stock boils, as it loses flavour if boiled for too long.

Right: Miso & Tofu Soup (top);
Shiitake & Egg Soup

Shiitake & Egg Soup

The delicate flavour of this clear soup goes well with any sushi.

Serves 4

INGREDIENTS
600 ml/1 pint/2½ cups Kombu Seaweed &
   Bonito Flake Stock or instant dashi
4 shiitake mushrooms, stems removed and
   thinly sliced
5 ml/1 tsp salt
10 ml/2 tsp usukuchi soy sauce
5 ml/1 tsp sake or dry white wine
2 small eggs
½ punnet cress, to garnish

1 Bring the stock to the boil, add the shiitake mushrooms and simmer for 1–2 minutes. Do not overcook. Add the salt, usukuchi soy sauce and sake or wine. Then break the eggs into a bowl and stir thoroughly with chopsticks.

2 Pour the eggs into the soup in a thin steady stream, in a circular motion – rather like drawing a spiral shape in the soup. To keep the soup clear, the heat must be high enough to set the egg as soon as it is added.

3 Simmer for a few seconds until the eggs are cooked. Use a pair of chopsticks to break up the egg, and divide the soup among four serving bowls. Sprinkle with cress and serve immediately.

Pork & Vegetable Soup

This soup has a distinctive and subtle flavour, which is easily lost if it is allowed to overcook.

Serves 4

INGREDIENTS
50 g/2 oz gobo (optional)
5 ml/1 tsp rice vinegar
½ black konnyaku, 125 g/4¼ oz
10 ml/2 tsp oil
200 g/7 oz belly pork, cut into thin
   3–4 cm/1¼–1½ in long strips
115 g/4 oz mooli, peeled and
   thinly sliced
50 g/2 oz carrot, thinly sliced
1 medium potato, thinly sliced
4 shiitake mushrooms, stems removed
   and thinly sliced
800 ml/27 fl oz/3½ cups
   Kombu Seaweed & Bonito Flake Stock
   or instant dashi
15 ml/1 tbsp sake or dry
   white wine
45 ml/3 tbsp red or white miso

FOR THE GARNISH
2 spring onions, thinly sliced
seven spice flavour

1 Scrub the skin off the gobo, if using, with a vegetable brush. Slice the vegetable into fine shavings. Soak the prepared gobo for 5 minutes in plenty of water with the vinegar added to remove any bitter taste, then drain.

2 Put the piece of konnyaku in a small pan and add enough water just to cover it. Bring to the boil over a moderate heat, then drain and allow to cool. Tear the konnyaku into 2 cm/ ¾ in lumps.

3 Heat the oil in a deep saucepan and quickly stir-fry the strips of pork. Add the gobo, if using, together with the mooli, carrot, potato, shiitake mushrooms and konnyaku, and stir-fry for 1 minute. Pour in the stock and sake or dry white wine.

4 Bring the soup to the boil, then skim it and allow it to simmer for 10 minutes, until the vegetables have softened.

VARIATIONS: If gobo is not available you could use other root vegetables such as turnip or celeriac.

5 Ladle a little of the soup into a small bowl and dissolve the miso in it. Pour the mixture back into the saucepan and bring to the boil once more. Remove from the heat, then pour into serving bowls. Sprinkle with the spring onions and seven spice flavour and serve immediately.

Mixed Vegetable Soup

The main ingredient for this soup is crushed tofu, which is both nutritious and satisfying.

Serves 4

INGREDIENTS
150 g/5 oz fresh tofu, weighed without water
2 dried shiitake mushrooms
50 g/2 oz gobo
5 ml/1 tsp rice vinegar
½ black or white konnyaku, 125 g/4¼ oz
30 ml/2 tbsp sesame oil
115 g/4 oz mooli, thinly sliced
50 g/2 oz carrot, thinly sliced
700 ml/24 fl oz/scant 3 cups Kombu Seaweed
   & Bonito Flake Stock or instant dashi
pinch of salt
30 ml/2 tbsp sake or dry white wine
7.5 ml/1½ tsp mirin
45 ml/3 tbsp white or red miso
dash of soy sauce
6 mangetouts, trimmed, boiled and thinly
   sliced, to garnish

1 Crush the tofu by hand until it resembles lumpy scrambled egg. Wrap in a dish towel and put it in a strainer, then pour over plenty of boiling water. Leave to drain for 10 minutes.

2 Soak the mushrooms in tepid water for 20 minutes, then drain them, reserving the liquid to add to the stock. Remove their stems, and cut the caps into 4–6 pieces.

3 Use a vegetable brush to scrub the skin off the gobo and slice it into thin shavings. Soak for 5 minutes in plenty of cold water with the vinegar added to remove any bitter taste. Drain well.

4 Put the konnyaku in a small saucepan and pour over just enough water to cover it. Bring to the boil, drain and allow to cool. Tear the konnyaku into 2 cm/¾ in lumps.

5 Heat the sesame oil in a deep saucepan. Add the shiitake mushrooms, gobo, mooli, carrot and konnyaku. Stir-fry for 1 minute, then add the tofu and stir well. Pour in the stock and add the salt, sake or wine and mirin. Bring to the boil. Skim the broth and simmer for 5 minutes.

6 In a bowl, dissolve the miso in a little of the soup, then return it to the pan. Simmer gently for 10 minutes, until the vegetables are soft.

7 Add the soy sauce, then remove from the heat. Serve immediately in four bowls, garnished with the sliced mangetouts.

Chilled Noodles

This classic Japanese dish of cold noodles is known as *Somen*. The noodles are surprisingly refreshing when eaten with the accompanying ingredients and a delicately flavoured dip.

Serves 4

INGREDIENTS
oil, for frying
2 eggs, beaten with a pinch of salt
1 sheet yaki-nori seaweed,
    finely shredded
½ bunch spring onions,
    thinly sliced
wasabi paste
400 g/14 oz dried somen noodles
ice cubes, for serving

FOR THE DIP
1 litre/1¾ pints/4 cups Kombu Seaweed &
    Bonito Flake Stock or instant dashi
200 ml/7 fl oz/scant 1 cup
    soy sauce
15 ml/1 tbsp mirin

1 First, prepare the dip. Bring all the ingredients to the boil in a medium saucepan, then remove from the heat. Allow to cool, then chill thoroughly.

2 Heat a little oil in a frying pan. Pour in half the egg, tilting the pan to coat the base evenly. Leave the egg to set, then turn it over and cook the second side briefly. Turn the omelette out on to a board. Cook the remaining egg in the same way.

3 Leave the omelettes to cool, then shred them finely. Divide the shredded omelette, nori, spring onions and wasabi among four individual bowls.

4 Boil the somen noodles according to the packet instructions and drain. Rinse the noodles in or under cold running water, stirring with chopsticks, then drain well.

COOK'S TIPS: Use scissors to shred the nori finely. Stir the noodles gently with chopsticks when rinsing them, as they are easily damaged.

5 Place the noodles on a large plate and add some ice cubes on top to keep them cool.

6 Pour the cold dip into four small bowls. Noodles and selected accompaniments are dipped into the chilled dip before they are eaten.

Five-flavour Noodles

The Japanese title, *Gomoku Yakisoba,* means five different ingredients but you can add as many different ingredients as you wish.

Serves 4

INGREDIENTS

500 g/1¼ lb fresh soba noodles or
 300 g/11 oz dried Chinese thin
 egg noodles
200 g/7 oz lean boneless pork,
 thinly sliced
20 ml/4 tsp oil
6 g/¼ oz fresh root ginger, grated
1 garlic clove, crushed
200 g/7 oz/1¾ cups green cabbage,
 roughly chopped
115 g/4 oz/½ cup beansprouts
1 green pepper, seeded and cut into
 fine strips
1 red pepper, seeded and cut into
 fine strips
salt and freshly ground
 white pepper
20 ml/4 tsp nori seaweed flakes,
 to garnish (optional)

FOR THE SEASONING

60 ml/4 tbsp Worcestershire sauce
15 ml/1 tbsp soy sauce
15 ml/1 tbsp oyster sauce
15 ml/1 tbsp sugar
2.5 ml/½ tsp salt

1 Boil the noodles according to the packet instructions and drain. Cut the pork into 3–4 cm/1¼–1½ in strips and season with salt and pepper.

2 Heat 7.5 ml/1½ tsp oil in a large frying pan or wok and stir-fry the pork until just cooked, then remove it from the pan.

3 Wipe the pan with kitchen paper, and then heat the remaining oil in it. Add the ginger, garlic and cabbage and stir-fry for 1 minute.

4 Add the beansprouts and stir until softened, then add the green and red peppers and stir-fry for 1 minute.

5 Return the pork to the pan and add the noodles. Stir in all the seasoning ingredients and season with white pepper. Stir-fry for 2–3 minutes. Serve immediately, sprinkled with the nori seaweed flakes (if using).

Mixed Rice

This recipe makes a very good party dish, and you can add a variety of ingredients to create your own special version.

Serves 4

INGREDIENTS
6 dried shiitake mushrooms
800 ml/27 fl oz/3½ cups water
2 sheets fried tofu, each
    13 x 6 cm/5 x 2½ in
6 mangetouts
1 carrot, cut into matchstick strips
115 g/4 oz chicken fillet, diced
30 ml/2 tbsp sugar
35 ml/7 tsp soy sauce
1 kg/2¼ lb/7 cups freshly
    boiled rice (450 g/1 lb/3½ cups raw)
salt

2 Put the fried tofu into a strainer and pour over hot water. Squeeze the tofu and cut it in half lengthways, then slice into 5 mm/¼ in wide strips.

3 Boil the mangetouts until just tender, drain and refresh in cold water and then drain well. Shred the mangetouts finely.

1 Soak the dried shiitake mushrooms in the water for 30 minutes. Place a small plate or saucer on top of the mushrooms to keep them submerged.

VARIATIONS: Other vegetables you might like to try include fried aubergines, peas, bamboo shoots and broad beans.

4 Drain the shiitake mushrooms, reserving the soaking water, remove their stems and finely slice the caps. Pour the soaking water into a saucepan. Add the carrot, chicken and shiitake mushrooms and tofu.

5 Bring to the boil, then skim the broth and simmer for 1–2 minutes. Add the sugar and cook for 1 minute, then add the soy sauce and salt. Simmer until most of the liquid has evaporated, leaving only a small amount of concentrated broth.

6 Mix in the hot rice, sprinkle the mangetouts over and serve the mixed rice at once.

Rice Triangles

Picnics are very popular in Japan. Various cooked meals are taken on picnics, including rice triangles, or *Onigiri*.

Serves 4

INGREDIENTS
15 ml/1 tbsp salt
1 kg/2¼ lb/7 cups freshly boiled
    Japanese rice (450 g/1 lb/3½ cups raw)
4 umeboshi
1 salmon steak, grilled
½ sheet yaki-nori seaweed
15 ml/1 tbsp white or black
    sesame seeds
cucumber and cress, to garnish

1 Put the salt in a bowl. Spoon an eighth of the rice into a small rice bowl. Make a hole in the middle and put in 1 umeboshi. Cover with rice.

COOK'S TIP: Always use hot rice to make the triangles, then allow them to cool completely and wrap each one in foil or clear film if taking on a picnic.

2 Wet the palms of both hands with cold water. Put a finger into the salt bowl and then rub the salt evenly on to your palms.

3 Empty the rice and umeboshi from the bowl on to one hand. Use both hands to shape the rice into a triangular shape, using firm but not heavy pressure. Make another three rice triangles in the same way.

4 Flake the salmon, discarding the skin and bones. Mix the fish into the remaining rice, then shape it into triangles as before.

5 Allow the triangles to cool. Cut the yaki-nori into four even strips and wrap a strip around each of the umeboshi rice triangles. Sprinkle sesame seeds on the salmon rice triangles and serve, garnished with cucumber and cress.

This edition published by Southwater

Distributed in the UK by
The Manning Partnership, 251-253 London Road East, Batheaston, Bath BA1 7RL, UK
tel. (0044) 01225 852 727   fax. (0044) 01225 852 852

Distributed in the USA by
Ottenheimer Publishing, 5 Park Center Court, Suite 300, Owing Mills MD 21 17-5001, USA
tel. (001) 410 902 9100   fax. (001) 410 902 7210

Distributed in Australia by
Sandstone Publishing, Unit 1, 360 Norton Street, Leichhardt, New South Wales 2040, Australia
tel. (0061) 2 9560 7888   fax. (0061) 2 9560 7488

Distributed in New Zealand by
Five Mile Press NZ, PO Box 33-1071, Takapuna
Auckland 9, New Zealand
tel. (0064) 9 4444 144 fax. (0064) 4444 518

A CIP catalogue record for this book
is available from the British Library.

Publisher: Joanna Lorenz
Editor: Valerie Ferguson
Series Designer: Bobbie Colgate Stone
Designer: Andrew Heath
Reader: Penelope Goodare
Production Controller: Joanna King
Recipes contributed by: Masaki Ko
Photography: Juliet Piddington

Notes:
For all recipes, quantities are given in
both metric and imperial measures and,
where appropriate, measures are also given
in standard cups and spoons.
Follow one set, but not a mixture, because they
are not interchangeable.
Standard spoon and cup measures are level.
1 tsp = 5 ml   1 tbsp = 15 ml
1 cup = 250 ml/8 fl oz
Australian standard tablespoons are 20 ml.
Australian readers should use 3 tsp in place of
1 tbsp for measuring small quantities of gelatine,
cornflour, salt, etc.
Medium eggs are used unless otherwise stated.

1 3 5 7 9 10 8 6 4 2

Printed and bound in Singapore